RADIANT
Reflections

**31-WEEK JOURNEY TO ILLUMINATE YOUR PATH
OF GROWTH AND TRANSFORMATION**

SUDECIA BROWN

Published by Brownstone Books
Boston, Massachusetts
September 2024

Copyright © 2024 by Sudecia Brown
All rights reserved.

Radiant Reflections: A 31-Week Journey to Illuminate Your
Path of Growth and Transformation

No part of this publication may be reproduced, distributed, or transmitted in any form or by any means, including photocopying, recording, or other electronic or mechanical methods, without the prior written permission of the publisher, except in the case of brief quotations embodied in critical reviews and certain other non-commercial uses permitted by copyright law.

ISBN: 979-8-9915417-2-5 (Paperback)
ISBN: 979-8-9915417-1-8 (Hardcover)
First Edition: November, 2024

Published by Brownstone Books Publishing
Boston, Massachusetts

Cover and interior design by Lisa Monias
Printed in United States of America

DEDICATION

"However long the night, the dawn will break."
— African Proverb

To my beloved mother, Isabelle Franklin-Brown, my "Senior Toddler Baby," This journal emerged from profound darkness and crisis. In my moments of despair, your powerful words illuminated my path: "Either you trust God or you don't. You are stronger than you think. Get up, shake the dust off you, move forward, and don't look back." Though you are no longer with me, your strength and wisdom resonate on every page. I dedicate this journal to you, Mom—your memory inspires me to rise with resilience and unwavering faith. You have shown me the essence of dignity and perseverance, and your spirit continues to shine brightly in my life.

I am deeply grateful to Bessie Storey, who I affectionately call, Mom, for your constant encouragement and acceptance. You always point me back to God. Dr. Cindy Trimm, my Life Strategist, your insightful guidance and transformative strategies empower me to navigate life's transitions with clarity and purpose. Thank you, Pastor Mona Thompson, for being my sister - your prayers and constant reminders of my victories strengthen me.

To my mentor, Casel Walker, your unwavering belief in me reinforces my sense of worth. Joanne Weintraub, you have been a bedrock of strength, offering unwavering support and empathy that helped me uncover my inner resilience. Carla Howze and Sandra Brown (my fam), your steadfast support has comforted me through life's storms. To my forever sisters from Fisk University, Patricia Williams and Valerie Waller, your belief in this journal inspired me to complete it. Dr. Tamika Jacques, your invaluable feedback has profoundly shaped this work.

Finally, to all my family, friends, and Brilliance Sisters, your love and faith have been the foundation of my journey. Thank you.

"If you want to go fast, go alone. If you want to go far, go together."
— African Proverb

Through this journal, I hope to share the strength and wisdom you have instilled in me with those who may need it just as much as I did.

TABLE OF CONTENTS

Introduction 1

Directions for Use 2

Purpose 3

WEEK ONE: Setting the Vision: A Blank Canvas for the Future 5

WEEK TWO: Planting Seeds of Intention: Nurturing Growth 11

WEEK THREE: Cultivating Gratitude: Blossoms of Thankfulness 17

WEEK FOUR: Harvesting Positivity: Reaping the Fruits of Optimism 23

WEEK FIVE: Tending to Self-Reflection: The Mirror of Personal Growth 29

WEEK SIX: Nourishing Relationships: Cultivating Connection 35

WEEK SEVEN: Transformative Response: Shaping Our Journey 41

WEEK EIGHT: Breaking Self-Imposed Limits: Unleashing Inner Strength 47

WEEK NINE: Elevating Altitude: The Power of Positive Attitude 53

WEEK TEN: Embracing: the Dance of Transformation 59

WEEK ELEVEN: Timeless Dreams: A Journey of Renewed Goals 65

WEEK TWELVE: Rising from Adversity: Embracing Resilience 71

WEEK THIRTEEN: Embarking on the Journey: The Power of the First Step 77

WEEK FOURTEEN: Courageous Continuity: Learning from Success and Failure ... 83

WEEK FIFTEEN: Dancing Through Change: Embracing Transformation 89

WEEK SIXTEEN: Rising to Life's Occasions: Embracing Purposeful Living 95

WEEK SEVENTEEN: Persistent Progress: Navigating Slow Growth with Determination 101

WEEK EIGHTEEN: Inherent Strength: Tapping into Your Inner Resources 107

WEEK NINETEEN: Unveiling Inner Brilliance: Recognizing Your Inherent Worth 113

WEEK TWENTY: Purposeful Work: Aligning Passion with Fulfillment.. 119

WEEK TWENTY ONE: Fearless Ascent: Conquering the Unknown 125

WEEK TWENTY TWO: Pathways of Purpose: Crafting Your Tomorrow................................... 131

WEEK TWENTY THREE: Heartfelt Convictions: The Power Within.. 137

WEEK TWENTY FOUR: Breaking Boundaries: Forging Paths... 143

WEEK TWENTY FIVE: Cultivating The Garden of Thought: Nurturing Positivity and Growth 149

WEEK TWENTY SIX: Navigating Crossroads: The Power of Choice 155

WEEK TWENTY SEVEN: Unveiling Destiny: A Journey of Conviction and Commitment 161

WEEK TWENTY EIGHT: Soaring Beyond Limits: Achieving Triumph in Audacious Goals .. 167

WEEK TWENTY NINE: Embracing Transformation: Navigating the Winds of Change........ 173

WEEK THIRTY: Exploring the Uncharted: Discovering Essence in New Paths...................... 179

WEEK THIRTY ONE: Unleashing Imagination: A Journey Beyond Boundaries 185

GUIDED MEDITATION : Inspire Your Thoughts And Aspirations 190

ABOUT THE AUTHOR: **SUDECIA BROWN** An Inspiring Educator, Minister, Speaker 191

INTRODUCTION

Welcome to "Radiant Reflections: A 31-Week Journey to Illuminate Your Path of Growth and Transformation." This journal is your companion on a purposeful expedition, inviting you to explore the depths of self-discovery, resilience, and positive transformation. Each day offers a chance to illuminate the corridors of your mind, unveiling the radiance within and paving the way for a more inspired and intentional life.

LET THIS JOURNAL BE YOUR GUIDE

As you embark on this radiant journey, I extend heartfelt gratitude for allowing "Radiant Reflections" to be part of your daily life. May each day within these pages bring you closer to the brilliant light within you. Thank you for choosing this journal as your guide, and may your path be illuminated with wisdom, joy, and a radiant transformation.

Thank You,
Sudecia Brown

DIRECTIONS FOR USE

1. Daily Dive: Begin each day by immersing yourself in the daily wisdom featuring Quote of the Day, Scripture of the Day, and daily prompts.

2. Reflect and Express: Engage with the reflections and Transcendence Writing Exercises, allowing your thoughts and experiences to flow onto these pages.

3. Take Purposeful Steps: Follow the daily Power Steps, making deliberate choices toward personal growth and positive change.

4. Nurture Creativity: Use the Transcendence Writing Exercises and Inventive Mindset Activities to spark your creativity and broaden your perspective.

5. Affirm Positivity: Reinforce positive beliefs with Elevated Consciousness Activities and Reflection Prompts, empowering your mindset.

6. Personalize Your Glow: Tailor the content to align with your unique goals and experiences, making this journey uniquely yours.

7. Craft a heartfelt letter to your most authentic self: This exercise encourages deep self-reflection and connection with your true essence, allowing you to articulate your values, dreams, and aspirations. It fosters self-acceptance and boosts confidence, inspiring you to align your actions with your genuine self. By putting your thoughts and feelings into words, you create a tangible reminder of who you are and who you aspire to be, serving as motivation on your personal growth journey.

PURPOSE

"Radiant Reflections" is crafted to be more than just a journal; it's a radiant compass guiding you towards self-illumination and growth. Through daily reflections, intentional actions, and creative exploration, this journey aims to deepen your awareness, foster resilience, and empower you to embrace new beginnings with an enlightened spirit. Let this journal catalyze positive transformation and create a life that radiates purpose.

The Cinematic Inspiration is a curated selection of movies to accompany you on your "Journey to Radiance." Just as your journal prompts and exercises aim to illuminate different facets of your inner self, these films have been carefully chosen to resonate with the daily themes and inspire reflection.

In the realm of storytelling, movies possess a unique power to evoke emotions, spark introspection, and convey profound messages. As you embark on this transformative journey, let these cinematic experiences be more than mere entertainment—they are mirrors reflecting aspects of your own narrative and windows opening to new perspectives.

Allow the characters, narratives, and visuals to intertwine with your reflections, enhancing the depth of your self-discovery. Each movie has its essence, contributing to the overarching theme of the day, Day, or month. Embrace the stories as you would a conversation with a wise friend, and let them enrich your understanding of the themes explored in your journal.

May the Cinematic Inspiration add an extra layer of depth to your "Journey to Radiance," elevating your experience and making every moment of introspection a cinematic celebration of your personal growth. Lights, camera, and let the journey begin!

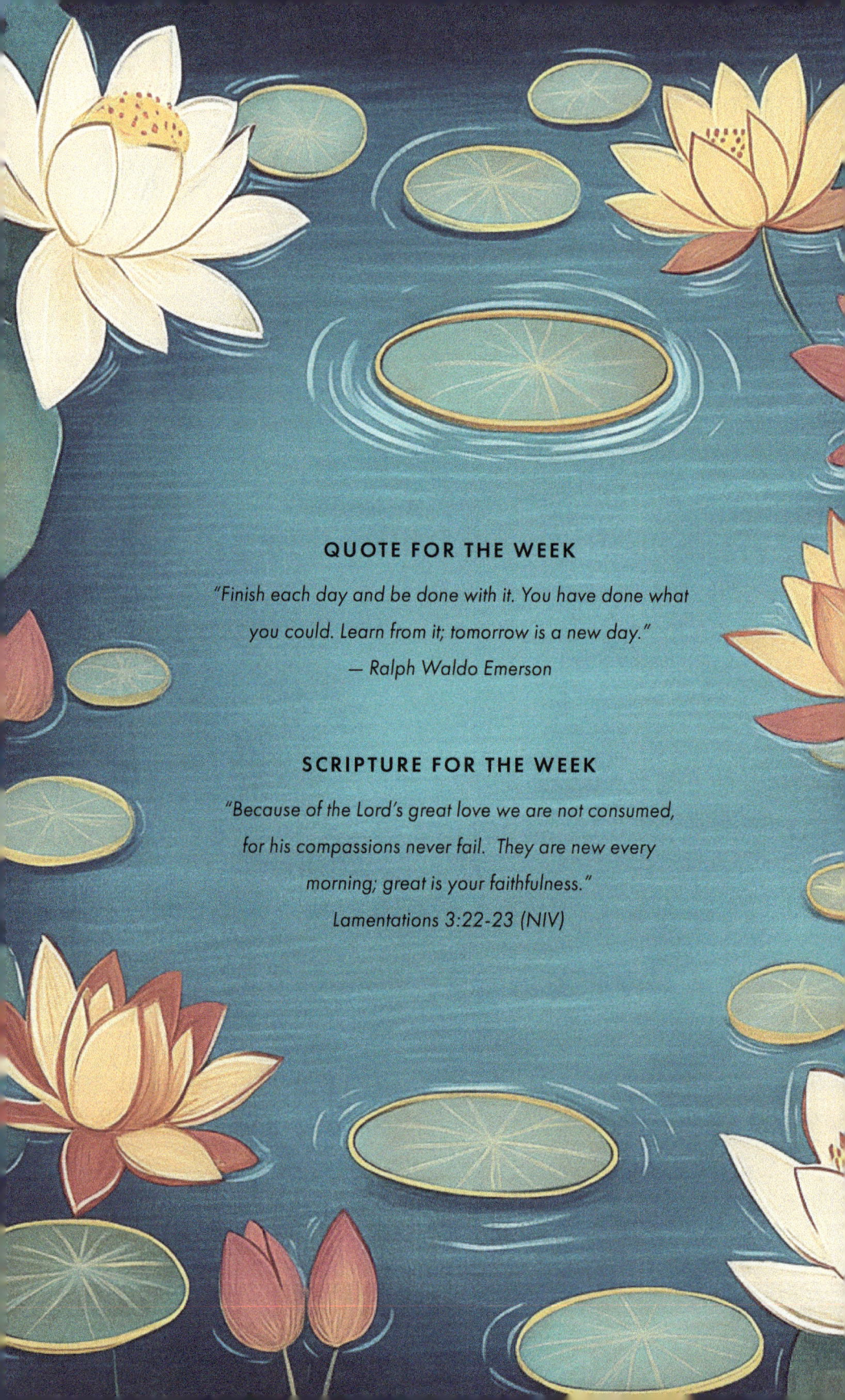

QUOTE FOR THE WEEK

"Finish each day and be done with it. You have done what you could. Learn from it; tomorrow is a new day."
— Ralph Waldo Emerson

SCRIPTURE FOR THE WEEK

"Because of the Lord's great love we are not consumed, for his compassions never fail. They are new every morning; great is your faithfulness."
Lamentations 3:22-23 (NIV)

WEEK ONE

Setting the Vision: A Blank Canvas for the Future

POWER STEPS THIS WEEK

Reflect on one thing you're grateful for this week, and let that sense of appreciation fill you with warmth and positivity, reminding you of the abundance of good in your life and inspiring you to spread kindness and gratitude to those around you.

Set a positive intention for today.

TRANSCENDENCE WRITING EXERCISE

Write about a time when embracing a new beginning led to unexpected and positive outcomes. Explore and list the emotions, challenges, and growth you experienced during that transition.

MY TRANSFORMATIONAL MOMENT

After facing potential job loss, I pursued my passion for advocacy and writing, which unexpectedly opened doors to creative opportunities and growth, both personally and professionally. Embracing change became a catalyst for transformation.

REFLECTION PROMPT

What is one small step you can take today to embrace a new beginning, no matter how intimidating it may seem?

INVENTIVE MINDSET ACTIVITY

Imagine your life as a book. If today were the beginning of a new chapter, what title would you give it, and what plot twists or adventures do you hope to encounter?

ELEVATED CONSCIOUSNESS ACTIVITY

List three positive affirmations that resonate with you and repeat them throughout the day to reinforce a mindset of embracing new beginnings.

Remember, each day is a fresh start. Clean your slate by embracing new beginnings and open yourself to a world of possibilities and growth.

CINEMATIC INSPIRATION
"The Secret Life of Walter Mitty" (2013) - Directed by Ben Stiller.

DESCRIPTION
"The Secret Life of Walter Mitty" follows the story of Walter Mitty, a daydreamer who escapes his mundane reality through vivid fantasies. When Walter embarks on a real-life adventure to recover a missing photograph, the film becomes a visual spectacle that mirrors the transformative power of setting a vision and embracing new possibilities.

How did the characters' experiences or choices resonate with your life journey, and what insights can you draw from your actions or dilemmas to enhance your personal growth?

In what ways did the themes or messages of the movie challenge your perspectives, beliefs, or assumptions about yourself and the world around you, and how can you integrate these reflections into your daily life to foster positive change?

LETTER TO MY AUTHENTIC SELF:
A CELEBRATION OF UNIQUENESS AND ASPIRATION

Craft a heartfelt letter to your most authentic self—the purest reflection of who you truly are and the person you strive to be. Pour out your thoughts, dreams, and aspirations, celebrating your uniqueness and embracing the journey toward your fullest potential.

Dear Authentic Self,

QUOTE FOR THE WEEK

"Every new beginning comes from some other beginning's end."
— Seneca the Younger

SCRIPTURE FOR THE WEEK

"Brothers and sisters, I do not consider myself yet to have taken hold of it. But one thing I do: Forgetting what is behind and straining toward what is ahead, I press on toward the goal to win the prize for which God has called me heavenward in Christ Jesus."
Philippians 3:13-14 (NIV)

WEEK TWO

Planting Seeds of Intention: Nurturing Growth

POWER STEPS THIS WEEK

Identify three areas of your life where you have hesitated to start anew.

What small actionable steps can you take toward that new beginning today?

TRANSCENDENCE WRITING EXERCISE

Describe a dream or goal you've put on hold. What steps can you take to reignite that aspiration and set a new beginning in motion?

MY TRANSFORMATIONAL MOMENT

After a long break, I reignited my aspiration for school leadership by enrolling in a post-graduate program and dedicating five hours a day for two years to meet state requirements. This journey reaffirmed the transformative power of consistent, incremental efforts and the value of staying committed.

INVENTIVE MINDSET ACTIVITY

What advice would you offer if you were a mentor guiding your past self through a significant life change? Consider the wisdom you've gained and how it can inspire a fresh start.

REFLECTION PROMPT

In what ways can embracing change contribute to your personal growth and fulfillment?

ELEVATED CONSCIOUSNESS ACTIVITY

Visualize yourself achieving a significant goal. What emotions and sensations accompany this success? Channel this positive energy throughout the day.

Treat each day as a fresh start. Set a small, achievable goal each morning aligned with your long-term aspirations, and reflect on your progress each evening for continuous growth.

CINEMATIC INSPIRATION
"The Tree of Life" (2011) - Directed by Terrence Malick.

DESCRIPTION
"The Tree of Life" is a poetic exploration of existence, nature, and the human experience. Through the lens of a family in 1950s Texas, the film intertwines the cosmic and the personal, symbolizing the planting of intentional and unintentional seeds that shape the characters' paths and influence their growth.

How did the characters' experiences or choices resonate with your life journey, and what insights can you draw from your actions or dilemmas to enhance your personal growth?

In what ways did the themes or messages of the movie challenge your perspectives, beliefs, or assumptions about yourself and the world around you, and how can you integrate these reflections into your daily life to foster positive change?

LETTER TO MY AUTHENTIC SELF:
A CELEBRATION OF UNIQUENESS AND ASPIRATION

Craft a heartfelt letter to your most authentic self—the purest reflection of who you truly are and the person you strive to be. Pour out your thoughts, dreams, and aspirations, celebrating your uniqueness and embracing the journey toward your fullest potential.

Dear Authentic Self,

QUOTE FOR THE WEEK

"Progress is impossible without change,
and those who cannot change their minds cannot change anything."
— George Bernard Shaw

SCRIPTURE FOR THE WEEK

"Forget the former things; do not dwell on the past.
See, I am doing a new thing! Now it springs up; do you not perceive it?
I am making a way in the wilderness and streams in the wasteland."
Isaiah 43:18-19

WEEK THREE

Cultivating Gratitude: Blossoms of Thankfulness

POWER STEPS THIS WEEK

Identify three habits you want to change. List reasons why you want to change them.

Replace these habits with positive actions and commit to changing them each day.

TRANSCENDENCE WRITING EXERCISE

Explore the concept of renewal in nature. How can the changing seasons serve as a metaphor for personal growth and embracing new beginnings?

MY TRANSFORMATIONAL MOMENT

Just as spring follows winter, I embraced the cycles of change in my life, recognizing that periods of stagnation are often followed by renewed energy and growth.

REFLECTION PROMPT

What can you let go of today to make space for something new and positive in your life?

INVENTIVE MINDSET ACTIVITY

Envision yourself as the architect of your ideal day. What activities, people, and experiences would you include to make it a perfect start to a new chapter?

ELEVATED CONSCIOUSNESS ACTIVITY

List three things you're excited about for the day, fostering a mindset of anticipation and positivity.

CINEMATIC INSPIRATION
"Amélie" (2001) - Directed by Jean-Pierre Jeunet.

DESCRIPTION
"Amélie" is a whimsical tale about a young woman who finds joy in small acts of kindness. As Amélie cultivates gratitude by positively impacting those around her, the film becomes a visual feast of whimsy and charm. It celebrates the beauty of gratitude and kindness and the profound impact of cultivating a thankful heart.

How did the characters' experiences or choices resonate with your life journey, and what insights can you draw from your actions or dilemmas to enhance your personal growth?

In what ways did the themes or messages of the movie challenge your perspectives, beliefs, or assumptions about yourself and the world around you? How can you integrate these reflections into your daily life to foster positive change?

LETTER TO MY AUTHENTIC SELF:
A CELEBRATION OF UNIQUENESS AND ASPIRATION

Craft a heartfelt letter to your most authentic self—the purest reflection of who you truly are and the person you strive to be. Pour out your thoughts, dreams, and aspirations, celebrating your uniqueness and embracing the journey toward your fullest potential.

Dear Authentic Self,

QUOTE FOR THE WEEK

"The journey of a thousand miles begins with one step."
— Lao Tzu

SCRIPTURE FOR THE WEEK

"Commit to the Lord whatever you do, and He will establish your plans."
Proverbs 16:3 (NIV)

WEEK FOUR

Harvesting Positivity: Reaping the Fruits of Optimism

POWER STEPS THIS WEEK

Define three short-term personal or professional goals.

Break them down into smaller, achievable tasks and complete one goal within two-Days.

TRANSCENDENCE WRITING EXERCISE

Reflect on a time when fear held you back from a new opportunity. How did you overcome it, and what positive outcomes resulted?

MY TRANSFORMATIONAL MOMENT

Despite my apprehension about interviewing for new opportunities, I embraced the chance to build my capacity by hiring a coach. Overcoming the initial discomfort led to increased confidence and unforeseen opportunities.

REFLECTION PROMPT

How can you turn a setback into a setup for a new beginning?

INVENTIVE MINDSET ACTIVITY

Imagine your life as a puzzle. What new piece could you add today to create a more complete and fulfilling picture?

ELEVATED CONSCIOUSNESS ACTIVITY

Affirm your ability to adapt and thrive in the face of challenges. Repeat and write affirmations that emphasize resilience and growth.

CINEMATIC INSPIRATION
"The Pursuit of Happyness" (2006) - Directed by Gabriele Muccino.

DESCRIPTION
Based on a true story, "The Pursuit of Happyness" portrays Chris Gardner's journey from homelessness to a successful career. The film is a testament to the power of optimism and determination, illustrating how a positive mindset can lead to the harvest of success even in the face of adversity.

How did the characters' experiences or choices resonate with your life journey, and what insights can you draw from your actions or dilemmas to enhance your personal growth?

In what ways did the themes or messages of the movie challenge your perspectives, beliefs, or assumptions about yourself and the world around you, and how can you integrate these reflections into your daily life to foster positive change?

LETTER TO MY AUTHENTIC SELF:
A CELEBRATION OF UNIQUENESS AND ASPIRATION

Craft a heartfelt letter to your most authentic self—the purest reflection of who you truly are and the person you strive to be. Pour out your thoughts, dreams, and aspirations, celebrating your uniqueness and embracing the journey toward your fullest potential.

Dear Authentic Self,

QUOTE FOR THE WEEK

"Keep your face always toward the sunshine
—and shadows will fall behind you."
— Walt Whitman

SCRIPTURE FOR THE WEEK

"Have I not commanded you? Be strong and courageous. Do not be afraid; do not be discouraged, for the Lord your God will be with you wherever you go."
Joshua 1:9 (NIV)

WEEK FIVE

Tending to Self-Reflection: The Mirror of Personal Growth

POWER STEPS THIS WEEK

Take a moment to ponder and craft your thoughts. Consider a fear or belief that may be holding you back.

Challenge it by taking a small action that contradicts that fear. Write it down and act on it.

TRANSCENDENCE WRITING EXERCISE

Explore the concept of courage. Write about a time when you displayed unexpected bravery and how it positively impacted your life.

MY TRANSFORMATIONAL MOMENT

Stepping into a leadership role was intimidating, but facing the challenge head-on enhanced my capacity, transferable skills and inspired confidence in those around me.

REFLECTION PROMPT

How can embracing discomfort lead to personal growth and empowerment?

INVENTIVE MINDSET ACTIVITY

Imagine you have a magic wand that can instantly remove one obstacle from your life. What would you eliminate, and how would it impact your journey of new beginnings?

ELEVATED CONSCIOUSNESS ACTIVITY

Envision your ideal self. What qualities and characteristics would you embody? Carry this vision with you throughout the day.

CINEMATIC INSPIRATION
"Good Will Hunting" (1997) - Directed by Gus Van Sant.

DESCRIPTION
"Good Will Hunting" delves into the transformative journey of Will Hunting, a janitor with a genius-level intellect. As Will navigates self-discovery through therapy, the film explores tending to self-reflection, facing past wounds, and fostering personal growth.

How did the characters' experiences or choices resonate with your life journey, and what insights can you draw from your actions or dilemmas to enhance your personal growth?

In what ways did the themes or messages of the movie challenge your perspectives, beliefs, or assumptions about yourself and the world around you, and how can you integrate these reflections into your daily life to foster positive change?

LETTER TO MY AUTHENTIC SELF:
A CELEBRATION OF UNIQUENESS AND ASPIRATION

Craft a heartfelt letter to your most authentic self—the purest reflection of who you truly are and the person you strive to be. Pour out your thoughts, dreams, and aspirations, celebrating your uniqueness and embracing the journey toward your fullest potential.

Dear Authentic Self,

QUOTE FOR THE WEEK

"Finish each day and be done with it. You have done what you could. Learn from it; tomorrow is a new day."
— Ralph Waldo Emerson

SCRIPTURE FOR THE WEEK

"Because of the Lord's great love we are not consumed, for his compassions never fail. They are new every morning; great is your faithfulness."
Lamentations 3:22-23 (NIV)

WEEK SIX

Nourishing Relationships: Cultivating Connection

POWER STEPS THIS WEEK

What passions or interests have sparked your curiosity but remain unexplored? Take a moment to jot them down.

What would your life look like if you fully embraced these passions? How might they contribute to your personal growth and fulfillment?

TRANSCENDENCE WRITING EXERCISE

Describe a moment when you felt in complete alignment with your passion. How can you incorporate more of this into your life?

MY TRANSFORMATIONAL MOMENT

Rediscovering my love for critical thinking and science brought me immense joy. Integrating this passion into my routine has since added a new layer of fulfillment to my life.

REFLECTION PROMPT

How can aligning your actions with your passions lead to a more purposeful and satisfying life?

INVENTIVE MINDSET ACTIVITY

If your life were a canvas, what colors and elements would you add today to make it more vibrant and meaningful?

ELEVATED CONSCIOUSNESS ACTIVITY

List three things you love about yourself. Celebrate these qualities throughout the day.

CINEMATIC INSPIRATION
"Big Fish" (2003) - Directed by Tim Burton.

DESCRIPTION
"Big Fish" is a heartwarming and visually enchanting film directed by Tim Burton. It explores themes of storytelling, imagination, and the complex relationships between fathers and sons. The movie's whimsical narrative and magical elements make it an excellent choice for a day focused on creativity in your "Journey to Radiance" journal.

How did the characters' experiences or choices resonate with your life journey, and what insights can you draw from your actions or dilemmas to enhance your personal growth?

In what ways did the themes or messages of the movie challenge your perspectives, beliefs, or assumptions about yourself and the world around you, and how can you integrate these reflections into your daily life to foster positive change?

LETTER TO MY AUTHENTIC SELF:
A CELEBRATION OF UNIQUENESS AND ASPIRATION

Craft a heartfelt letter to your most authentic self—the purest reflection of who you truly are and the person you strive to be. Pour out your thoughts, dreams, and aspirations, celebrating your uniqueness and embracing the journey toward your fullest potential.

Dear Authentic Self,

QUOTE FOR THE WEEK

"In the middle of difficulty lies opportunity."
— Albert Einstein

SCRIPTURE FOR THE WEEK

"Do not conform to the pattern of this world, but be transformed by the renewing of your mind. Then you will be able to test and approve what God's will is—his good, pleasing, and perfect will."
Romans 12:2 (NIV)

WEEK SEVEN

Transformative Response: Shaping Our Journey

POWER STEPS THIS WEEK

Reflect on a recent challenge or setback you encountered. What did you learn from the experience?

Focus on finding a positive lesson or opportunity within that experience. Write it down.

TRANSCENDENCE WRITING EXERCISE

Reflect on the concept of resilience. Write about a time when you bounced back from adversity more robustly and wisely.

MY TRANSFORMATIONAL MOMENT

Experiencing a career crisis taught me the importance of adaptability. Embracing change led to a better mindset, a transition in career fits, and a more fulfilling professional journey.

REFLECTION PROMPT

How can shifting your perspective empower you to face challenges with resilience and optimism?

INVENTIVE MINDSET ACTIVITY

If you could rewrite the narrative of a challenging experience, how would you reinterpret it to highlight growth and triumph?

ELEVATED CONSCIOUSNESS ACTIVITY

Affirm your ability to navigate challenges. Write and speak affirmations that emphasize your resilience and capacity for positive adaptation.

CINEMATIC INSPIRATION

A Beautiful Mind" (2001) - Directed by Ron Howard.

DESCRIPTION

"A Beautiful Mind" aligns with the theme of transformative responses and finding positive opportunities amid challenges. The film tells the true story of John Nash (played by Russell Crowe), a brilliant mathematician who faces mental health challenges. Despite the difficulties, Nash learns to navigate his condition, eventually finding a renewed sense of purpose and making significant contributions to his field. The movie explores the transformative power of resilience, positive thinking, and the ability to find beauty and opportunities despite adversity.

How did the characters' experiences or choices resonate with your life journey, and what insights can you draw from your actions or dilemmas to enhance your personal growth?

In what ways did the themes or messages of the movie challenge your perspectives, beliefs, or assumptions about yourself and the world around you, and how can you integrate these reflections into your daily life to foster positive change?

LETTER TO MY AUTHENTIC SELF:
A CELEBRATION OF UNIQUENESS AND ASPIRATION

Craft a heartfelt letter to your most authentic self—the purest reflection of who you truly are and the person you strive to be. Pour out your thoughts, dreams, and aspirations, celebrating your uniqueness and embracing the journey toward your fullest potential.

Dear Authentic Self,

QUOTE FOR THE WEEK

"The greatest mistake you can make in life is to be continually fearing you will make one."
— Elbert Hubbard

SCRIPTURE FOR THE WEEK

"I can do all this through him who gives me strength."
Philippians 4:13 (NIV)

WEEK EIGHT

Breaking Self-Imposed Limits: Unleashing Inner Strength

POWER STEPS THIS WEEK

Recognize a self-imposed limit or belief that may be holding you back. What is it, and how has it affected your growth?

In what ways can you reframe this belief into a more empowering perspective, and how could that shift impact your actions moving forward?

TRANSCENDENCE WRITING EXERCISE

Reflect on a time when you faced a self-imposed limit or belief that hindered your progress. Describe the steps you took to challenge and overcome this limitation. How did your confidence in yourself contribute to your success? Explore the concept of self-belief and its impact on your journey.

MY TRANSFORMATIONAL MOMENT

Overcoming self-doubt allowed me to pursue a challenging project. The experience boosted my skills and shattered limiting beliefs about my capabilities.

REFLECTION PROMPT

How can breaking through self-imposed limits lead to personal growth and expanded possibilities?

INVENTIVE MINDSET ACTIVITY

What opportunities would open up if you could remove one barrier in your life? Visualize, imagine, and write down your new horizons and opportunities.

ELEVATED CONSCIOUSNESS ACTIVITY

Affirm your unlimited potential. Speak aloud and write down a slogan reinforcing your belief in your capabilities.

CINEMATIC INSPIRATION
"Rocky" (1976) - Directed by John G. Avildsen.

DESCRIPTION
"Rocky" tells the inspirational story of Rocky Balboa, an underdog boxer who seizes an unexpected chance to challenge the heavyweight champion. Overcoming self-doubt and societal expectations, Rocky breaks through his perceived limitations through intense training, determination, and belief in his potential. The film powerfully illustrates the transformative journey of inner strength and resilience, serving as a motivational reminder that our greatest limits are often self-imposed.

How did the characters' experiences or choices resonate with your life journey, and what insights can you draw from your actions or dilemmas to enhance your personal growth?

In what ways did the themes or messages of the movie challenge your perspectives, beliefs, or assumptions about yourself and the world around you, and how can you integrate these reflections into your daily life to foster positive change?

LETTER TO MY AUTHENTIC SELF:
A CELEBRATION OF UNIQUENESS AND ASPIRATION

Craft a heartfelt letter to your most authentic self—the purest reflection of who you truly are and the person you strive to be. Pour out your thoughts, dreams, and aspirations, celebrating your uniqueness and embracing the journey toward your fullest potential.

Dear Authentic Self,

QUOTE FOR THE WEEK

"Whether you think you can, or you think you can't—you're right."
— Henry Ford

SCRIPTURE FOR THE WEEK

"Above all else, guard your heart, for everything you do flows from it."
Proverbs 4:23 (NIV)

WEEK NINE

Elevating Altitude: The Power of Positive Attitude

POWER STEPS THIS WEEK

Reflect on the idea of "Elevating Altitude: The Power of Positive Attitude" and jot down your thoughts on how it influences your life.

_____
_____
_____
_____
_____
_____
_____

Replace any negative thoughts with positive affirmations. What affirmations resonate with you?

_____
_____
_____
_____
_____
_____
_____
_____

TRANSCENDENCE WRITING EXERCISE

Recall a time when a positive mindset transformed a challenging situation. How did your attitude shape the outcome? Reflect on how optimism helps you navigate difficulties and enhances your overall well-being and success. How can you apply this mindset to future challenges?

MY TRANSFORMATIONAL MOMENT

Approaching a difficult conversation with optimism diffused tension and led to a constructive resolution, showcasing the power of a positive attitude.

REFLECTION PROMPT

How can maintaining a positive attitude improve your well-being and relationships?

INVENTIVE MINDSET ACTIVITY

If your mind were a garden, what seeds would you plant today to cultivate a more positive and fruitful mindset?

ELEVATED CONSCIOUSNESS ACTIVITY

Begin and end your day with a positive affirmation. Reflect, notice and write how it influences your perspective throughout the day.

CINEMATIC INSPIRATION
The Blind Side" (2009) - Directed by John Lee Hancock.

DESCRIPTION
The movie is based on the true story of Michael Oher, a homeless teenager taken in by a caring family, the Tuohys. Sandra Bullock plays Leigh Anne Tuohy, who plays a crucial role in Michael's life. The film explores compassion, resilience, and the transformative power of positive influence. Leigh Anne Tuohy's positive attitude and determination to help Michael impact his life and highlight the potential for positive change when one person chooses to make a difference.

How did the characters' experiences or choices resonate with your life journey, and what insights can you draw from your actions or dilemmas to enhance your personal growth?

In what ways did the themes or messages of the movie challenge your perspectives, beliefs, or assumptions about yourself and the world around you, and how can you integrate these reflections into your daily life to foster positive change?

LETTER TO MY AUTHENTIC SELF:
A CELEBRATION OF UNIQUENESS AND ASPIRATION

Craft a heartfelt letter to your most authentic self—the purest reflection of who you truly are and the person you strive to be. Pour out your thoughts, dreams, and aspirations, celebrating your uniqueness and embracing the journey toward your fullest potential.

Dear Authentic Self,

QUOTE FOR THE WEEK

"The only thing that is constant is change."
— Heraclitus

SCRIPTURE FOR THE WEEK

"There is a time for everything and a season for every activity under the heavens."
Ecclesiastes 3:1 (NIV)

WEEK TEN

Embracing: the Dance of Transformation

POWER STEPS THIS WEEK

Embrace a change you've been resisting. Reflect and write about it.

Identify one positive aspect or opportunity that comes with this change.

TRANSCENDENCE WRITING EXERCISE

Write about the concept of embracing uncertainty. Share a personal story where navigating the unknown led to positive outcomes.

MY TRANSFORMATIONAL MOMENT

Facing an unexpected employment crisis tested my resilience and opened doors to new opportunities. By embracing uncertainty, I uncovered hidden strengths and adapted through networking and upskilling. This journey not only helped me overcome challenges but also boosted my confidence in navigating life's unpredictability. This journal stands as a testament to my growth and a source of inspiration for future endeavors.

REFLECTION PROMPT

How can embracing change, even when uncomfortable, lead to personal, professional and spiritual growth?

INVENTIVE MINDSET ACTIVITY

Imagine change as a dance. What unique steps can you add to make the dance of change more graceful and enjoyable?

ELEVATED CONSCIOUSNESS ACTIVITY

Affirm your ability to adapt and thrive in the face of change. Create, write and speak new affirmations that reinforce your resilience.

CINEMATIC INSPIRATION
"Eat Pray Love" (2010) - Directed by Ryan Murphy.

DESCRIPTION
"Eat Pray Love" aligns with the theme of embracing change and finding positive opportunities within it. The film follows Elizabeth Gilbert, played by Julia Roberts, on a journey of self-discovery as she embraces significant life changes. Each phase of her journey, from Italy to India and finally to Indonesia, represents a different season of transformation. The movie beautifully captures the idea that by plunging into change, one can move with it and find new, buoyant rhythms in the dance of life.

How did the characters' experiences or choices resonate with your life journey, and what insights can you draw from your actions or dilemmas to enhance your personal growth?

In what ways did the themes or messages of the movie challenge your perspectives, beliefs, or assumptions about yourself and the world around you, and how can you integrate these reflections into your daily life to foster positive change?

LETTER TO MY AUTHENTIC SELF:
A CELEBRATION OF UNIQUENESS AND ASPIRATION

Craft a heartfelt letter to your most authentic self—the purest reflection of who you truly are and the person you strive to be. Pour out your thoughts, dreams, and aspirations, celebrating your uniqueness and embracing the journey toward your fullest potential.

Dear Authentic Self,

QUOTE FOR THE WEEK

"It is never too late to be what you might have been."
— George Eliot

SCRIPTURE FOR THE WEEK

For I know the plans I have for you," declares the Lord, "plans to prosper you and not to harm you, plans to give you hope and a future."
Jeremiah 29:11 (NIV)

WEEK ELEVEN

Timeless Dreams: A Journey of Renewed Goals

POWER STEPS THIS WEEK

Write about the dream or goal you've deferred. What inspired it? Why did you set it aside? What would pursuing it look like now?

Develop a plan to reignite that dream. What steps can you take to move forward? Set specific, achievable goals.

TRANSCENDENCE WRITING EXERCISE

Consider the concept of lifelong learning. Write about a time when acquiring a new skill or knowledge opened unexpected doors in your life.

MY TRANSFORMATIONAL MOMENT

Embracing the challenge of learning a musical instrument provided a new skill and introduced me to a community of like-minded individuals.

REFLECTION PROMPT

How can adopting a continuous learning mindset enhance your personal and professional life?

INVENTIVE MINDSET ACTIVITY

If you could attend a workshop on any topic, what would it be, and how might it contribute to your personal growth?

ELEVATED CONSCIOUSNESS ACTIVITY

Affirm your openness to new possibilities. Repeat an affirmation that emphasizes your readiness to embrace change.

CINEMATIC INSPIRATION
The Bucket List" (2007) - Directed by Rob Reiner.

DESCRIPTION
"The Bucket List" features Morgan Freeman and Jack Nicholson as two terminally ill men on a journey to fulfill their lifelong dreams. The film beautifully highlights the importance of pursuing aspirations, regardless of age, and the transformative power of setting meaningful goals. As they explore their bucket lists, viewers are inspired to reflect on their own dreams and take action to achieve them.

How did the characters' experiences or choices resonate with your life journey, and what insights can you draw from your actions or dilemmas to enhance your personal growth?

In what ways did the themes or messages of the movie challenge your perspectives, beliefs, or assumptions about yourself and the world around you, and how can you integrate these reflections into your daily life to foster positive change?

LETTER TO MY AUTHENTIC SELF:
A CELEBRATION OF UNIQUENESS AND ASPIRATION

Craft a heartfelt letter to your most authentic self—the purest reflection of who you truly are and the person you strive to be. Pour out your thoughts, dreams, and aspirations, celebrating your uniqueness and embracing the journey toward your fullest potential.

Dear Authentic Self,

QUOTE FOR THE WEEK

"The darkest hour has only sixty minutes."
— Morris Mandel

SCRIPTURE FOR THE WEEK

"The Lord makes firm the steps of the one who delights in him; though he may stumble, he will not fall, for the Lord upholds him with his hand."
Psalms 37:23-24 (NIV)

WEEK TWELVE

Rising from Adversity: Embracing Resilience

POWER STEPS THIS WEEK

Reflect on a recent mistake or failure. What insights can you gain from this experience?

Identify three concrete actions you can take to apply these insights and move forward.

TRANSCENDENCE WRITING EXERCISE

Explore the theme of resilience. Write about a time when perseverance through challenges led to a meaningful accomplishment.

MY TRANSFORMATIONAL MOMENT

Despite setbacks, completing a complex project showcased my determination and resilience, leading to personal and professional recognition.

REFLECTION PROMPT

How can viewing failure as a positive stepping stone to success change your approach to challenges?

INVENTIVE MINDSET ACTIVITY

What bold steps would you take today to achieve your goals if you saw failure as a valuable opportunity for growth?

ELEVATED CONSCIOUSNESS ACTIVITY

Affirm your resilience in the face of challenges. Create, write, and speak affirmations that reinforce your ability to overcome obstacles.

CINEMATIC INSPIRATION
"Whale Rider" (2002) -Directed by Niki Caro.

DESCRIPTION
The story is set in a Maori community in New Zealand and follows a young girl named Paikea, played by Keisha Castle-Hughes, who aspires to become the leader of her tribe despite facing gender-based challenges and resistance from traditional elders. The movie beautifully depicts Paikea's resilience, determination, and strength in adversity. Her journey to prove herself and connect with her cultural heritage becomes a powerful narrative of overcoming challenges and rising above societal expectations.

How did the characters' experiences or choices resonate with your life journey, and what insights can you draw from your actions or dilemmas to enhance your personal growth?

In what ways did the themes or messages of the movie challenge your perspectives, beliefs, or assumptions about yourself and the world around you, and how can you integrate these reflections into your daily life to foster positive change?

LETTER TO MY AUTHENTIC SELF:
A CELEBRATION OF UNIQUENESS AND ASPIRATION

Craft a heartfelt letter to your most authentic self—the purest reflection of who you truly are and the person you strive to be. Pour out your thoughts, dreams, and aspirations, celebrating your uniqueness and embracing the journey toward your fullest potential.

Dear Authentic Self,

QUOTE FOR THE WEEK

"The journey of a thousand miles begins with one step."
— Lao Tzu

SCRIPTURE FOR THE WEEK

"Trust in the Lord with all your heart and lean not on your own understanding; in all your ways submit to him, and he will make your paths straight." Proverbs 3:5-6 (NIV)

WEEK THIRTEEN

Embarking on the Journey: The Power of the First Step

POWER STEPS THIS WEEK

Identify a long-term goal or dream. Why is it important to you, and how would achieving it impact your life?

Reflect on the first step you can take to move closer to this goal, and outline a plan to get started.

TRANSCENDENCE WRITING EXERCISE

Consider the concept of trust. Write about a time when trusting yourself or others led to positive outcomes.

MY TRANSFORMATIONAL MOMENT

Trusting a colleague with a crucial task strengthened our professional relationship and resulted in a successful project.

REFLECTION PROMPT

How can trust in yourself and others contribute to your journey of embracing new beginnings?

INVENTIVE MINDSET ACTIVITY

If you could travel to any place right now, where would you go, and how might the experience inspire new beginnings?

ELEVATED CONSCIOUSNESS ACTIVITY

Affirm your trust in the journey. Create, write and speak affirmations that reinforce your confidence in the path you're on.

CINEMATIC INSPIRATION
"Wild" (2014) - Directed by Jean-Marc Vallée.

DESCRIPTION
Based on Cheryl Strayed's memoir, "Wild" follows her transformative hike along the Pacific Crest Trail, as she seeks healing and self-discovery. Reese Witherspoon's performance highlights the challenges and triumphs of taking that first step into the unknown. The film explores themes of resilience, personal growth, and the power of embarking on a life-changing journey, sparking discussions about the importance of preparation and self-awareness.

How did the characters' experiences or choices resonate with your life journey, and what insights can you draw from your actions or dilemmas to enhance your personal growth?

In what ways did the themes or messages of the movie challenge your perspectives, beliefs, or assumptions about yourself and the world around you, and how can you integrate these reflections into your daily life to foster positive change?

LETTER TO MY AUTHENTIC SELF:
A CELEBRATION OF UNIQUENESS AND ASPIRATION

Craft a heartfelt letter to your most authentic self—the purest reflection of who you truly are and the person you strive to be. Pour out your thoughts, dreams, and aspirations, celebrating your uniqueness and embracing the journey toward your fullest potential.

Dear Authentic Self,

QUOTE FOR THE WEEK

"Success is not final, failure is not fatal: It is the courage to continue that counts." — Winston Churchill

SCRIPTURE FOR THE WEEK

"For the Spirit God gave us does not make us timid, but gives us power, love, and self-discipline."
2 Timothy 1:7 (NIV)

WEEK FOURTEEN

Courageous Continuity: Learning from Success and Failure

POWER STEPS THIS WEEK

Reflect on a past success that aligns with your current goals. How did courage and perseverance help you then, and how can you apply those lessons to move forward now?

Identify one key factor that contributed to that success and consider how to apply it to a current challenge.

TRANSCENDENCE WRITING EXERCISE

Explore the theme of courage. Write about a time when facing a fear or taking a bold step led to positive change.

MY TRANSFORMATIONAL MOMENT

Confronting a fear of public speaking enhanced my communication skills and opened up opportunities for leadership roles.

REFLECTION PROMPT

How can cultivating courage in your actions contribute to personal and professional growth?

INVENTIVE MINDSET ACTIVITY

If you had a superpower, what would it be, and how would you use it to create positive change in your life?

ELEVATED CONSCIOUSNESS ACTIVITY

Affirm your courage and strength. Create, write and speak affirmations that reinforce your ability to overcome challenges.

CINEMATIC INSPIRATION
Unbroken" (2014) - Directed by Angelina Jolie.

DESCRIPTION
"Unbroken" tells the true story of Louis Zamperini, an Olympian and WWII veteran, who survives a plane crash, drifting at sea, and harsh conditions as a POW. The film highlights his resilience and determination, illustrating courage in the face of adversity. It's a powerful testament to the human spirit's ability to endure, showing how both successes and failures contribute to personal growth and triumph over hardship.

How did the characters' experiences or choices resonate with your life journey, and what insights can you draw from your actions or dilemmas to enhance your personal growth?

In what ways did the themes or messages of the movie challenge your perspectives, beliefs, or assumptions about yourself and the world around you, and how can you integrate these reflections into your daily life to foster positive change?

LETTER TO MY AUTHENTIC SELF:
A CELEBRATION OF UNIQUENESS AND ASPIRATION

Craft a heartfelt letter to your most authentic self—the purest reflection of who you truly are and the person you strive to be. Pour out your thoughts, dreams, and aspirations, celebrating your uniqueness and embracing the journey toward your fullest potential.

Dear Authentic Self,

QUOTE FOR THE WEEK

"To live is the rarest thing in the world. Most people exist, that is all."
— *Oscar Wilde*

SCRIPTURE FOR THE WEEK

There is a time for everything, and a season for every activity under the heavens; a time to be born and a time to die, a time to plant and a time to uproot, a time to kill and a time to heal, a time to tear down and a time to build, a time to weep and a time to laugh, a time to mourn and a time to dance, a time to scatter stones and a time to gather them, a time to embrace and a time to refrain from embracing,

Ecclesiastes 3:1-5 (NIV)

WEEK FIFTEEN

Dancing Through Change: Embracing Transformation

POWER STEPS THIS WEEK

Identify an area in your life where change is necessary.

Take a proactive step towards embracing change, whether big or small, by identifying one specific action you can take today that aligns with your goals and executing it with intention and purpose.

TRANSCENDENCE WRITING EXERCISE

Reflect on the concept of adaptability. Recall a specific instance where your flexibility led to positive outcomes. How can you leverage this experience to propel yourself toward your goals? Carefully consider how you can apply this lesson to your own goals.

MY TRANSFORMATIONAL MOMENT

By staying open-minded and flexible, I navigated uncertainties with resilience and creativity. I viewed obstacles as opportunities for growth and incorporated adaptability into my goal-setting. This approach helped me stay focused and responsive, increasing my chances of success.

REFLECTION PROMPT

How can being open-minded about change enhance your personal and professional life?

INVENTIVE MINDSET ACTIVITY

If you could time travel to any period in your life, what advice would your future self give you to navigate change effectively?

ELEVATED CONSCIOUSNESS ACTIVITY

Affirm your adaptability. Create, write and speak affirmations that reinforce your openness to change.

CINEMATIC INSPIRATION
"La La Land" (2016) - Directed by Damien Chazelle.

DESCRIPTION
The film follows the story of aspiring actress Mia and jazz musician Sebastian as they navigate the challenges of pursuing their dreams in the vibrant city of Los Angeles. The movie's musical and visual elements capture the essence of life as a dance, with its ebbs and flows, ups and downs, and the beauty of embracing change. "La La Land" is an inspiring and visually stunning portrayal of the transformative power of pursuing one's passions and navigating the changes that come with it.

How did the characters' experiences or choices resonate with your life journey, and what insights can you draw from your actions or dilemmas to enhance your personal growth?

In what ways did the themes or messages of the movie challenge your perspectives, beliefs, or assumptions about yourself and the world around you, and how can you integrate these reflections into your daily life to foster positive change?

LETTER TO MY AUTHENTIC SELF:
A CELEBRATION OF UNIQUENESS AND ASPIRATION

Craft a heartfelt letter to your most authentic self—the purest reflection of who you truly are and the person you strive to be. Pour out your thoughts, dreams, and aspirations, celebrating your uniqueness and embracing the journey toward your fullest potential.

Dear Authentic Self,

QUOTE FOR THE WEEK

"The future belongs to those who believe in the beauty of their dreams."
— Eleanor Roosevelt

SCRIPTURE FOR THE WEEK

"For I know the plans I have for you, declares the Lord, plans for welfare and not for evil, to give you a future and a hope."
Jeremiah 29:11

WEEK SIXTEEN

Rising to Life's Occasions: Embracing Purposeful Living

POWER STEPS THIS WEEK

Embrace the transformative potential of reflection by setting aside 15 minutes today to journal about your life journey. Write about the unique opportunities for growth and evolution you've encountered along the way.

Identify one aspect where you can rise to the occasion and positively impact today, then reflect on your life journey, journaling about how taking action in this area aligns with your personal growth and aspirations.

TRANSCENDENCE WRITING EXERCISE

Reflect on a significant moment in your life when you felt a profound sense of purpose and direction. Consider the emotions, people, and events that shaped this experience and how it influenced your identity, relationships, and aspirations. As you contemplate your journey forward, explore actionable steps you can take to align your daily actions with your sense of purpose, nurturing greater fulfillment and connection in your life.

MY TRANSFORMATIONAL MOMENT

During a difficult time, I found solace in praying for my chronically ill mother. Sitting by her bedside, I felt a deep sense of purpose and peace. This experience shaped my understanding of empathy, showing me the power of prayer to bring hope and healing.

REFLECTION PROMPT

Reflect on a significant moment in your life when you felt a profound sense of purpose and direction. Consider the emotions, people, and events that shaped this experience and how it influenced your identity, relationships, and aspirations. As you contemplate your journey forward, explore actionable steps you can take to align your daily actions with your sense of purpose, nurturing greater fulfillment and connection in your life.

INVENTIVE MINDSET ACTIVITY

What achievements would be highlighted if you could attend a celebration in your honor, and how might this inspire new beginnings?

ELEVATED CONSCIOUSNESS ACTIVITY

After creating an affirmation, how can you pair it with specific actions to align with your evolving purpose? For example, if your affirmation is "I embrace my evolving purpose with courage," what tangible steps can you take each day to explore new opportunities or gain clarity on your passions and values?

CINEMATIC INSPIRATION
"Dead Poets Society" (1989) - Directed by Peter Weir.

DESCRIPTION
"Dead Poets Society" aligns with the theme of rising to life's occasions and embracing purposeful living. The film, set in an elite boys' prep school, follows an English teacher, John Keating (played by Robin Williams), who inspires his students to seize the day and live authentically. The movie encourages viewers to reflect on the significance of their actions, the pursuit of passion, and their impact on the world. "Dead Poets Society" is a powerful reminder of the transformative potential when individuals rise to the occasions presented.

How did the characters' experiences or choices resonate with your life journey, and what insights can you draw from your actions or dilemmas to enhance your personal growth?

In what ways did the themes or messages of the movie challenge your perspectives, beliefs, or assumptions about yourself and the world around you, and how can you integrate these reflections into your daily life to foster positive change?

LETTER TO MY AUTHENTIC SELF:
A CELEBRATION OF UNIQUENESS AND ASPIRATION

Craft a heartfelt letter to your most authentic self—the purest reflection of who you truly are and the person you strive to be. Pour out your thoughts, dreams, and aspirations, celebrating your uniqueness and embracing the journey toward your fullest potential.

Dear Authentic Self,

QUOTE FOR THE WEEK

"Perseverance is not a long race; it is many short races one after the other."
— Walter Elliot

SCRIPTURE FOR THE WEEK

Let us not become weary in doing good,
for at the proper time we will reap a harvest if we do not give up."
Galatians 6:9 (NIV)

WEEK SEVENTEEN

Persistent Progress: Navigating Slow Growth with Determination

POWER STEPS THIS WEEK

Reflect on a goal that feels like it's progressing slowly. Consider why progress might be sluggish and identify any obstacles or challenges in your way.

Brainstorm potential strategies for overcoming these obstacles and accelerating progress toward your goal. Remember to stay patient and focused, and take small steps forward each day. Commit to persisting with a tiny action today despite any challenges.

TRANSCENDENCE WRITING EXERCISE

Reflect on a significant challenge you've faced, whether a major obstacle or a recent setback. Describe the emotions and strategies you used to overcome it, and how your perseverance shaped the outcome. Finally, explore how your mindset influenced your response to these challenges and what lessons you've learned about resilience for future endeavors."

MY TRANSFORMATIONAL MOMENT

Losing my mother brought overwhelming grief, but to heal and honor her, I leaned on my faith, loved ones, nature walks, and journaling, finding strength and solace through each.

REFLECTION PROMPT

How can maintaining momentum in your pursuits lead to long-term success?

INVENTIVE MINDSET ACTIVITY

Imagine you had the opportunity to sit down with your past self during a challenging period. What advice or words of encouragement would you offer to inspire them to persevere through the difficulties they were facing? Think creatively about the wisdom you would share and how it could positively impact your past experiences

ELEVATED CONSCIOUSNESS ACTIVITY

Strengthen your persistence with an empowering affirmation. Stand in front of a mirror, repeat and record a powerful statement that reinforces your commitment to keep moving forward, such as "I am resilient and capable of overcoming any obstacle" or "With every challenge, I grow stronger and more determined.

CINEMATIC INSPIRATION
"Moneyball" (2011) - Directed by Bennett Miller.

DESCRIPTION
"Moneyball" embodies persistent progress and determination amid challenges, telling the true story of Billy Beane, the Oakland A's general manager (played by Brad Pitt), who builds a competitive team on a limited budget. Despite resistance, Beane's unconventional methods revolutionized baseball scouting. The film highlights the power of persistence, innovation, and strategic thinking in achieving success.

How did the characters' experiences or choices resonate with your life journey, and what insights can you draw from your actions or dilemmas to enhance your personal growth?

In what ways did the themes or messages of the movie challenge your perspectives, beliefs, or assumptions about yourself and the world around you, and how can you integrate these reflections into your daily life to foster positive change?

LETTER TO MY AUTHENTIC SELF:
A CELEBRATION OF UNIQUENESS AND ASPIRATION

Craft a heartfelt letter to your most authentic self—the purest reflection of who you truly are and the person you strive to be. Pour out your thoughts, dreams, and aspirations, celebrating your uniqueness and embracing the journey toward your fullest potential.

Dear Authentic Self,

QUOTE FOR THE WEEK

"Believe you can and you're halfway there." — Theodore Roosevelt

SCRIPTURE FOR THE WEEK

"No temptation has overtaken you except what is common to mankind. And God is faithful; he will not let you be tempted beyond what you can bear. But when you are tempted, he will also provide a way out so that you can endure it." 1 Corinthians 10:13 (NIV)

WEEK EIGHTEEN

Inherent Strength: Tapping into Your Inner Resources

POWER STEPS THIS WEEK

Take a moment to reflect on a recent challenge you've encountered. Whether it's a personal, professional, or emotional obstacle, consider the specific circumstances, emotions, and thoughts associated with this challenge.

After reflecting on the challenge, identify three internal resources or strengths within yourself that you can leverage to overcome it. This could be resilience, determination, creativity, empathy, or any other inherent quality you possess. Consider how you can tap into this resource to navigate through the challenge with confidence and resilience.

TRANSCENDENCE WRITING EXERCISE

Reflect on what inner strength means to you and the qualities you rely on during challenges. Define inner strength and how it manifests in your life. Recall a specific instance when you used this inner strength to overcome a challenge.

How did leveraging your inner strength contribute to your resilience in adversity?

MY TRANSFORMATIONAL MOMENT

Amid a work crisis that left me defeated, I faced a pivotal test of resilience. By tapping into empathy, communication, and problem-solving, I navigated the challenge with grace and integrity, ultimately allowing inner strength—not circumstances—to define me.

REFLECTION PROMPT

How can recognizing and utilizing your internal resources empower you to face life's challenges?

INVENTIVE MINDSET ACTIVITY

Imagine your personal strengths as superpowers. List your strengths and visualize each one as a unique ability you can call upon in times of need. For each strength, write a brief description of how you would use it to overcome a specific challenge in your life. Reflect on how this imaginative exercise shifts your perspective on your strengths and the obstacles you face.

ELEVATED CONSCIOUSNESS ACTIVITY

Elevate your mindset and reinforce your inner strength by integrating a daily practice of affirming a potent statement, carefully craft a statement to instill unwavering confidence in your capabilities and resilience.

CINEMATIC INSPIRATION
"The Shawshank Redemption" (1994) - Directed by Frank Darabont.

DESCRIPTION
"The Shawshank Redemption" aligns with the theme by portraying the transformative power of inner strength and resilience. The film follows Andy Dufresne (played by Tim Robbins), a man wrongly convicted of murder, as he navigates the challenges of prison life. Despite the harsh circumstances, Andy relies on his inner resources to maintain hope, integrity, and a sense of purpose. The movie beautifully illustrates that even in adversity, individuals can tap into their inner strength to persevere and find redemption.

How did the characters' experiences or choices resonate with your life journey, and what insights can you draw from your actions or dilemmas to enhance your personal growth?

In what ways did the themes or messages of the movie challenge your perspectives, beliefs, or assumptions about yourself and the world around you, and how can you integrate these reflections into your daily life to foster positive change?

LETTER TO MY AUTHENTIC SELF:
A CELEBRATION OF UNIQUENESS AND ASPIRATION

Craft a heartfelt letter to your most authentic self—the purest reflection of who you truly are and the person you strive to be. Pour out your thoughts, dreams, and aspirations, celebrating your uniqueness and embracing the journey toward your fullest potential.

Dear Authentic Self,

QUOTE FOR THE WEEK

"What lies behind us and what lies before us are tiny matters compared to what lies within us." - Ralph Waldo Emerson.

SCRIPTURE FOR THE WEEK

"I praise you because I am fearfully and wonderfully made; your works are wonderful, I know that full well." Psalm 139:14 (NIV)

WEEK NINETEEN

Unveiling Inner Brilliance: Recognizing Your Inherent Worth

POWER STEPS THIS WEEK

Set aside 15 minutes today to reflect on a past success. Write about a specific moment when you felt proud of your accomplishment, detailing the event, your actions, and the outcome. Focus on the positive feelings and fulfillment that accompanied this success.

Identify one personal quality or skill that contributed to your success. Write it down and create a positive affirmation, such as "My perseverance and creativity are my strengths." Repeat this affirmation daily to reinforce your self-worth. Additionally, consider one way to leverage this quality in your current pursuits and take a small, actionable step to do so today.

TRANSCENDENCE WRITING EXERCISE

Consider the concept of self-appreciation. Reflect on a time when acknowledging your strengths and abilities enhanced your confidence. Describe the situation, the strengths or abilities you recognized in yourself, and how this self-appreciation positively impacted your confidence and actions.

MY TRANSFORMATIONAL MOMENT

Recognizing my analytical skills transformed my career, enhancing my decision-making and confidence. Each challenge I faced strengthened my clarity and drive, empowering me to embrace new opportunities and navigate uncertainties with resilience.

REFLECTION PROMPT

How can acknowledging and celebrating your unique qualities contribute to your journey of embracing new beginnings?

INVENTIVE MINDSET ACTIVITY

If you had a personal mascot representing your strengths, what would it be, and how might it inspire confidence in challenging situations?

ELEVATED CONSCIOUSNESS ACTIVITY

Affirm your unique qualities. Repeat a mantra that reinforces your appreciation for the strengths within you.

CINEMATIC INSPIRATION
"Akeelah and the Bee" (2006) - Directed by Doug Atchison.

DESCRIPTION
The film tells the story of Akeelah Anderson, a young girl with a natural talent for spelling. As she competes in spelling bees, the movie explores themes of self-discovery, confidence-building, and recognizing one's inherent worth. "Akeelah and the Bee" is an excellent choice for a film that emphasizes the idea that individuals possess unique talents and qualities within themselves, and through self-discovery and perseverance, they can recognize and unleash their inner brilliance.

How did the characters' experiences or choices resonate with your life journey, and what insights can you draw from your actions or dilemmas to enhance your personal growth?

In what ways did the themes or messages of the movie challenge your perspectives, beliefs, or assumptions about yourself and the world around you, and how can you integrate these reflections into your daily life to foster positive change?

LETTER TO MY AUTHENTIC SELF:
A CELEBRATION OF UNIQUENESS AND ASPIRATION

Craft a heartfelt letter to your most authentic self—the purest reflection of who you truly are and the person you strive to be. Pour out your thoughts, dreams, and aspirations, celebrating your uniqueness and embracing the journey toward your fullest potential.

Dear Authentic Self,

QUOTE FOR THE WEEK

"Choose a job you love, and you will never have to work a day in your life."
— Confucius

SCRIPTURE FOR THE WEEK

"Whatever you do, work at it with all your heart, as working for the Lord, not for human masters." - Colossians 3:23 (NIV)

WEEK TWENTY

Purposeful Work: Aligning Passion with Fulfillment

POWER STEPS THIS WEEK

Take 15 minutes to reflect on your passions. Write down three activities or interests that truly excite and motivate you. Consider how these passions can be incorporated into your work or daily life.

Choose one passion and identify a concrete action to integrate it into your work or a side project, such as starting a new initiative or learning a related skill. Write down your plan and take the first step today. Also, identify one aspect you can improve to better align with your values and goals.

TRANSCENDENCE WRITING EXERCISE

Explore the theme of fulfillment. Reflect on a time when aligning your work with your passions led to deep satisfaction. Describe the experience, the passions you integrated into your work, and how this alignment brought you a sense of purpose and contentment.

MY TRANSFORMATIONAL MOMENT

Choosing a career in education was a heartfelt calling fueled by my passion for learning. Every day in the classroom reaffirms my purpose, as I guide eager minds and nurture a love for learning. Despite challenges, the fulfillment and impact make it all worthwhile.

REFLECTION PROMPT

In what ways does aligning your daily activities with your values enrich and deepen the satisfaction and meaning in your life?

INVENTIVE MINDSET ACTIVITY

If you could design your ideal job or activity, what elements would it include, and how might this inspire positive change?

ELEVATED CONSCIOUSNESS ACTIVITY

Affirm your commitment to meaningful work. Create, write and speak an affirmation or reflection reinforcing your dedication to work that aligns with your values. For example, "Every decision I make aligns with my values and leads me towards a purposeful and fulfilling life."

CINEMATIC INSPIRATION
Hidden Figures" (2016) - Directed by Theodore Melfi

DESCRIPTION
"Hidden Figures" is a biographical drama that reveals the untold story of three African-American women mathematicians—Katherine Johnson, Dorothy Vaughan, and Mary Jackson—who played crucial roles at NASA during the 1960s Space Race. The film highlights their contributions to key missions, including John Glenn's historic orbit, while exploring themes of dedication and perseverance against systemic racism and gender bias. It celebrates the brilliance of these unsung heroes and their pivotal impact on space exploration.

How did the characters' experiences or choices resonate with your life journey, and what insights can you draw from your actions or dilemmas to enhance your personal growth?

In what ways did the themes or messages of the movie challenge your perspectives, beliefs, or assumptions about yourself and the world around you, and how can you integrate these reflections into your daily life to foster positive change?

LETTER TO MY AUTHENTIC SELF:
A CELEBRATION OF UNIQUENESS AND ASPIRATION

Craft a heartfelt letter to your most authentic self—the purest reflection of who you truly are and the person you strive to be. Pour out your thoughts, dreams, and aspirations, celebrating your uniqueness and embracing the journey toward your fullest potential.

Dear Authentic Self,

QUOTE FOR THE WEEK

"Do the thing you fear, and the death of fear is certain." — Ralph Waldo Emerson

SCRIPTURE FOR THE WEEK

"So do not fear, for I am with you; do not be dismayed, for I am your God. I will strengthen you and help you; I will uphold you with my righteous right hand." Isaiah 41:10 (NIV)

WEEK TWENTY ONE

Fearless Ascent: Conquering the Unknown

POWER STEPS THIS WEEK

Identify a fear that has been holding you back. Write down this fear and reflect on how it has impacted your life. Consider why this fear exists and how it limits your potential.

Break this fear into smaller, manageable steps. Create a list of these steps and take the first one today. Write down your action plan and reflect on how it feels to confront this fear, acknowledging your progress along the way.

TRANSCENDENCE WRITING EXERCISE

Consider the theme of courage. Write about a time when facing a fear led to personal growth and positive change.

MY TRANSFORMATIONAL MOMENT

Overcoming my fear of public speaking improved my communication skills and opened doors to leadership opportunities.

REFLECTION PROMPT

How can reframing your relationship with fear empower you to embrace new opportunities and experiences?

INVENTIVE MINDSET ACTIVITY

If fear were a puzzle, what pieces would you rearrange to turn it into a source of motivation and growth?

ELEVATED CONSCIOUSNESS ACTIVITY

Affirm your courage in the face of fear. Repeat a mantra that reinforces your ability to confront and overcome fears.

CINEMATIC INSPIRATION
"Life of Pi" (2012) - Directed by Ang Lee

DESCRIPTION
The film follows Pi Patel, a young Indian man who survives a shipwreck in the Pacific Ocean. Stranded on a lifeboat with a Bengal tiger named Richard Parker, Pi confronts his deepest fears and navigates the uncharted waters of the vast ocean. As Pi faces survival challenges, the movie explores themes of resilience, faith, and the transformative power of confronting one's fears. The breathtaking visuals and allegorical storytelling make "Life of Pi" a captivating exploration of the unknown and a testament to the strength found within.

How did the characters' experiences or choices resonate with your life journey, and what insights can you draw from your actions or dilemmas to enhance your personal growth?

In what ways did the themes or messages of the movie challenge your perspectives, beliefs, or assumptions about yourself and the world around you, and how can you integrate these reflections into your daily life to foster positive change?

LETTER TO MY AUTHENTIC SELF:
A CELEBRATION OF UNIQUENESS AND ASPIRATION

Craft a heartfelt letter to your most authentic self—the purest reflection of who you truly are and the person you strive to be. Pour out your thoughts, dreams, and aspirations, celebrating your uniqueness and embracing the journey toward your fullest potential.

Dear Authentic Self,

QUOTE FOR THE WEEK

"Life isn't about finding yourself. Life is about creating yourself."
— George Bernard Shaw

SCRIPTURE FOR THE WEEK

"Forget the former things; do not dwell on the past. See, I am doing a new thing! Now it springs up; do you not perceive it? I am making a way in the wilderness and streams in the wasteland." Isaiah 43:18-19 (NIV)

WEEK TWENTY TWO

Pathways of Purpose: Crafting Your Tomorrow

POWER STEPS THIS WEEK

Spend a few minutes each day visualizing yourself achieving your long-term goals. Imagine living the life you desire and experiencing fulfillment. Jot down your thoughts and feelings during this visualization.

Each morning, review your goals and create a list of action items that align with them. Prioritize tasks that will have the greatest impact on moving you closer to your vision for the future. Focus on completing these tasks throughout the day.

TRANSCENDENCE WRITING EXERCISE

Explore the concept of intention. Write about a time when setting a clear intention led to positive outcomes.

MY TRANSFORMATIONAL MOMENT

Realizing self-care was essential, I committed to it and saw profound changes in my energy, relationships, and work. This choice allowed me to show up fully, bringing purpose and focus to every interaction and task.

REFLECTION PROMPT

How can setting clear intentions guide your actions and decisions toward a more purposeful future?

INVENTIVE MINDSET ACTIVITY

If you were the author of your future story, what plot twists or adventures would you include to create a compelling narrative?

ELEVATED CONSCIOUSNESS ACTIVITY

Affirm your power to shape your future by writing and speaking affirmations that reinforce your ability to create the life you desire, such as "I am capable and worthy of achieving my dreams." Make this a daily practice, visualizing your success and feeling empowered with each repetition.

CINEMATIC INSPIRATION

"Soul" (2020), an animated film produced by Pixar Animation Studios, directed by Pete Docter and Kemp Powers.

DESCRIPTION

The story follows Joe Gardner, a middle school music teacher and aspiring jazz musician, on a metaphysical adventure in the afterlife. As he navigates between realms, Joe discovers the true essence of life, purpose, and the beauty of embracing every moment. Aligning with the theme of "Pathways of Purpose," "Soul" emphasizes the exploration of one's calling and invites viewers to reflect on finding purpose in both ordinary and extraordinary aspects of life.

How did the characters' experiences or choices resonate with your life journey, and what insights can you draw from your actions or dilemmas to enhance your personal growth?

In what ways did the themes or messages of the movie challenge your perspectives, beliefs, or assumptions about yourself and the world around you, and how can you integrate these reflections into your daily life to foster positive change?

LETTER TO MY AUTHENTIC SELF:
A CELEBRATION OF UNIQUENESS AND ASPIRATION

Craft a heartfelt letter to your most authentic self—the purest reflection of who you truly are and the person you strive to be. Pour out your thoughts, dreams, and aspirations, celebrating your uniqueness and embracing the journey toward your fullest potential.

Dear Authentic Self,

QUOTE FOR THE WEEK

"Believe you can, and you're halfway there."
—Theodore Roosevelt.

SCRIPTURE FOR THE WEEK

"Everything is possible for one who believes."
Mark 9:23 (NIV)

WEEK TWENTY THREE

Heartfelt Convictions: The Power Within

POWER STEPS THIS WEEK

Identify a goal or aspiration you want to achieve. Reflect deeply on why this goal is important to you and how it aligns with your values and aspirations. Visualize yourself accomplishing this goal and the positive impact it will have on your life.

Break down the goal into smaller, manageable steps and create a timeline for completion. Write down each step needed to achieve your goal and assign deadlines to each one. By breaking it down into smaller tasks, you make the goal less daunting and increase your likelihood of success.

TRANSCENDENCE WRITING EXERCISE

Reflect on the theme of belief. Write about a specific time when believing in yourself or others led to a significant success. What challenges did you face, and how did this belief influence your actions and outcomes? Consider the emotions involved and the lessons learned from this experience.

MY TRANSFORMATIONAL MOMENT

Amid an employment crisis that threatened my finances, my faith in God and core values became my anchor. Trusting His plan and holding to my principles gave me strength, helping me navigate economic turmoil with resilience and integrity.

REFLECTION PROMPT

How can cultivating a solid belief in yourself and your abilities contribute to your journey of embracing new beginnings?

INVENTIVE MINDSET ACTIVITY

If belief were a catalyst for innovation, what obstacles would you infuse it into today to foster positive transformation?

ELEVATED CONSCIOUSNESS ACTIVITY

Affirm your belief in your abilities. Create positive self-talk that reinforce your confidence and positive outlook.

CINEMATIC INSPIRATION
"The Power of the Heart" (2014) - Directed by Drew Heriot.

DESCRIPTION
"The Power of the Heart" is a compelling documentary by Drew Heriot that explores the profound connection between the heart, mind, and spirit. Featuring insights from spiritual leaders and scientists, it showcases how aligning beliefs with the wisdom of the heart can lead to personal transformation and growth. The film invites viewers to tap into their innate heart power to navigate life's challenges with resilience, authenticity, and purpose.

How did the characters' experiences or choices resonate with your life journey, and what insights can you draw from your actions or dilemmas to enhance your personal growth?

In what ways did the themes or messages of the movie challenge your perspectives, beliefs, or assumptions about yourself and the world around you, and how can you integrate these reflections into your daily life to foster positive change?

LETTER TO MY AUTHENTIC SELF:
A CELEBRATION OF UNIQUENESS AND ASPIRATION

Craft a heartfelt letter to your most authentic self—the purest reflection of who you truly are and the person you strive to be. Pour out your thoughts, dreams, and aspirations, celebrating your uniqueness and embracing the journey toward your fullest potential.

Dear Authentic Self,

QUOTE FOR THE WEEK

"The only limit to our realization of tomorrow is our doubts of today."
— Franklin D. Roosevelt

SCRIPTURE FOR THE WEEK

"Forget the former things; do not dwell on the past."
Isaiah 43:18 (NIV)

WEEK TWENTY FOUR

Breaking Boundaries: Forging Paths

POWER STEPS THIS WEEK

Reflect on three meaningful accomplishments you've achieved and write them down. Consider a pivotal lesson from your past that has shaped your personal growth and guided your future endeavors.

Brainstorm actionable steps to integrate this lesson into your daily life. Write specific ways to leverage this insight to enhance your growth and propel you toward your goals.

TRANSCENDENCE WRITING EXERCISE

Reflect on the theme of personal evolution. Describe a specific moment of growth and how it shaped your present self.

MY TRANSFORMATIONAL MOMENT

Conquering my fear of public speaking not only improved my communication skills but also significantly bolstered my self-confidence, showcasing the profound impact of personal growth.

REFLECTION PROMPT

How can acknowledging and celebrating your growth empower you to face future challenges confidently?

INVENTIVE MINDSET ACTIVITY

Reflect on your past self and envision what guidance you would offer during challenging times. What insights or strategies would you share to help navigate those difficulties more effectively?

ELEVATED CONSCIOUSNESS ACTIVITY

List three qualities you admire in yourself and allow them to guide your actions throughout the day.

CINEMATIC INSPIRATION
"Dune" (2021) - Directed by Denis Villeneuve.

DESCRIPTION
"Dune" is a visually stunning sci-fi epic directed by Denis Villeneuve. Set in the desert world of Arrakis, the film follows Paul Atreides as he confronts political intrigue and mystical challenges. Breaking societal boundaries, Paul transforms into a leader, exploring themes of destiny and courage. With breathtaking visuals and a rich narrative, "Dune" invites viewers to reflect on breaking free from established norms.

How did the characters' experiences or choices resonate with your life journey, and what insights can you draw from your actions or dilemmas to enhance your personal growth?

_____
_____
_____
_____

In what ways did the themes or messages of the movie challenge your perspectives, beliefs, or assumptions about yourself and the world around you, and how can you integrate these reflections into your daily life to foster positive change?

_____
_____
_____
_____

LETTER TO MY AUTHENTIC SELF:
A CELEBRATION OF UNIQUENESS AND ASPIRATION

Craft a heartfelt letter to your most authentic self—the purest reflection of who you truly are and the person you strive to be. Pour out your thoughts, dreams, and aspirations, celebrating your uniqueness and embracing the journey toward your fullest potential.

Dear Authentic Self,

QUOTE FOR THE WEEK

"The happiness of your life depends upon the quality of your thoughts."
— Marcus Aurelius

SCRIPTURE FOR THE WEEK

"For as he thinks in his heart, so is he."
Proverbs 23:7 (NIV)

WEEK TWENTY FIVE

Cultivating The Garden of Thought: Nurturing Positivity & Growth

POWER STEPS THIS WEEK

Allocate specific times during the day to consciously identify any negative thoughts or emotions you experience. Take a few minutes to jot them down. What's causing the thoughts?

For each negative thought or emotion recorded, provide a thoughtful positive affirmation and outline a specific action to address it. Additionally, craft three affirmations or actions that reflect an empowering attitude, reinforcing your commitment to personal growth.

TRANSCENDENCE WRITING EXERCISE

Reflect on the influence of your attitude. Describe a situation where a positive attitude transformed your experience.

MY TRANSFORMATIONAL MOMENT

Amid an employment crisis that threatened my finances, my faith in God and core values became my anchor. Trusting His plan and holding to my principles gave me strength, helping me navigate economic turmoil with resilience and integrity.

REFLECTION PROMPT

How can cultivating a positive attitude impact your interactions, relationships, and overall well-being?

INVENTIVE MINDSET ACTIVITY

If your attitude had a color, what color would it be today? How can you infuse more of that color into your thoughts and actions?

ELEVATED CONSCIOUSNESS ACTIVITY

If your attitude had a color, what color would it be today? How can you infuse more of that color into your thoughts and actions? How does this impact your mindset and interactions with others?

CINEMATIC INSPIRATION
"CODA" - Directed by Sian Heder.

DESCRIPTION
"CODA" is a heartwarming and inspiring film that follows Ruby, the only hearing member of a deaf family. As she navigates her unique identity, the movie explores themes of communication, understanding, and the transformative power of embracing one's true self.

How did the characters' experiences or choices resonate with your life journey, and what insights can you draw from your actions or dilemmas to enhance your personal growth?

In what ways did the themes or messages of the movie challenge your perspectives, beliefs, or assumptions about yourself and the world around you, and how can you integrate these reflections into your daily life to foster positive change?

LETTER TO MY AUTHENTIC SELF: A CELEBRATION OF UNIQUENESS AND ASPIRATION

Craft a heartfelt letter to your most authentic self—the purest reflection of who you truly are and the person you strive to be. Pour out your thoughts, dreams, and aspirations, celebrating your uniqueness and embracing the journey toward your fullest potential.

Dear Authentic Self,

QUOTE FOR THE WEEK

"The best way out is always through." — Robert Frost

SCRIPTURE FOR THE WEEK

"Whether you turn to the right or to the left, your ears will hear a voice behind you, saying, 'This is the way; walk in it." Isaiah 30:21 (NIV)

WEEK TWENTY SIX

Navigating Crossroads: The Power of Choice

POWER STEPS THIS WEEK

Pause for a moment of introspection and identify a significant challenge that currently confronts you in your life's journey. Reflect on it and write it down.

Having identified the challenge, deliberately choose a positive direction for addressing it, emphasizing growth and breakthrough in your approach. Meditate on it and write it down.

TRANSCENDENCE WRITING EXERCISE

Reflect on the concept of challenges as opportunities. Write about a time when facing a challenge led to a breakthrough and positive transformation.

MY TRANSFORMATIONAL MOMENT

During a challenging time, I was forced to leave my job, prompting me to enroll in a Data Analytics program. This decision broadened my knowledge and connected me with inspiring individuals, showing that embracing change fosters personal growth and new opportunities.

REFLECTION PROMPT
How can viewing challenges as opportunities for breakthroughs shift your perspective and approach?

INVENTIVE MINDSET ACTIVITY
If your challenges were stepping stones, where would they lead you? Envision the path to your breakthrough and write it down.

ELEVATED CONSCIOUSNESS ACTIVITY
Affirm your ability to choose a positive direction. Repeat a phrase that reinforces your commitment to growth and breakthroughs. Write it down.

CINEMATIC INSPIRATION
"Moneyball" (2011) - Directed by Bennett Miller.

DESCRIPTION
"Moneyball" is a gripping sports drama following Billy Beane, the GM of the Oakland Athletics, as he challenges baseball norms by adopting innovative strategies. Focusing on data-driven decisions and undervalued players, Beane reshapes the team's fortunes. The film explores the power of unconventional choices, resilience, and navigating crossroads. Through its compelling narrative and outstanding performances, "Moneyball" is a metaphor for life's challenges, prompting reflections on strategic decision-making and breakthroughs.

How did the characters' experiences or choices resonate with your life journey, and what insights can you draw from your actions or dilemmas to enhance your personal growth?

In what ways did the themes or messages of the movie challenge your perspectives, beliefs, or assumptions about yourself and the world around you, and how can you integrate these reflections into your daily life to foster positive change?

LETTER TO MY AUTHENTIC SELF:
A CELEBRATION OF UNIQUENESS AND ASPIRATION

Craft a heartfelt letter to your most authentic self—the purest reflection of who you truly are and the person you strive to be. Pour out your thoughts, dreams, and aspirations, celebrating your uniqueness and embracing the journey toward your fullest potential.

Dear Authentic Self,

QUOTE FOR THE WEEK

"Imagination is more important than knowledge. For knowledge is limited, whereas imagination embraces the entire world, stimulating progress, giving birth to evolution."
— Albert Einstein

SCRIPTURE FOR THE WEEK

Trust in the Lord with all your heart and lean not on your own understanding; in all your ways submit to him, and he will make your paths straight." Proverbs 3:5-6 (NIV)

WEEK TWENTY SEVEN

Unveiling Destiny: A Journey of Conviction and Commitment

POWER STEPS THIS WEEK

Take a moment to reflect on your ability to choose a positive direction in your life. Consider the areas where you want to see growth and breakthroughs, write them down.

Choose a phrase or affirmation that resonates with your commitment to growth and breakthroughs. Repeat this affirmation regularly throughout your day to reinforce your positive direction and commitment to personal development.

TRANSCENDENCE WRITING EXERCISE

Reflect on the power of conviction. Write about a time when unwavering belief in your dreams propelled you forward.

MY TRANSFORMATIONAL MOMENT

Reflecting on the power of conviction, I recall a challenging period in my career when my unwavering belief in my dreams drove me forward despite setbacks and doubts. I stayed committed to my vision of success, determined to pursue my goals.

REFLECTION PROMPT

How can strengthening your conviction empower you and align you with your path? Identify actionable steps to deepen your commitment to fulfilling this aspiration.

INVENTIVE MINDSET ACTIVITY

If your dreams were a destination, what steps would you take today to move closer to them?

ELEVATED CONSCIOUSNESS ACTIVITY

Affirm your unwavering belief in your dreams. Repeat a declaration that reinforces your conviction and commitment to your vision.

CINEMATIC INSPIRATION
"King Richard" (2021) - Directed by Reinaldo Marcus Green

DESCRIPTION
"King Richard" is an inspiring biographical drama that follows the extraordinary journey of Richard Williams, the father and coach of Venus and Serena Williams. Determined to see his daughters succeed in the competitive world of professional tennis, Richard faces numerous challenges and overcomes obstacles, emphasizing the power of commitment, unwavering conviction, and the pursuit of excellence. The film beautifully captures the resilience of a family and the untold story behind the rise of two tennis legends.

How did the characters' experiences or choices resonate with your life journey, and what insights can you draw from your actions or dilemmas to enhance your personal growth?

In what ways did the themes or messages of the movie challenge your perspectives, beliefs, or assumptions about yourself and the world around you, and how can you integrate these reflections into your daily life to foster positive change?

LETTER TO MY AUTHENTIC SELF:
A CELEBRATION OF UNIQUENESS AND ASPIRATION

Craft a heartfelt letter to your most authentic self—the purest reflection of who you truly are and the person you strive to be. Pour out your thoughts, dreams, and aspirations, celebrating your uniqueness and embracing the journey toward your fullest potential.

Dear Authentic Self,

QUOTE FOR THE WEEK

"Success is not final, failure is not fatal: It is the courage to continue that counts."
— Winston Churchill

SCRIPTURE FOR THE WEEK

But those who hope in the Lord will renew their strength. They will soar on wings like eagles; they will run and not grow weary, they will walk and not faint."
Isaiah 40:31 (NIV)

WEEK TWENTY EIGHT

Soaring Beyond Limits: Achieving Triumph in Audacious Goals

POWER STEPS THIS WEEK

Take a few moments to reflect on a goal that excites you and pushes your boundaries. Write down this goal, describing why it inspires you and how it challenges your limits. What emotions does it evoke?

Identify three actionable steps you can take to move closer to this goal. These steps can be small or large, but they should push you out of your comfort zone. Write down your plan and commit to taking the first step today.

TRANSCENDENCE WRITING EXERCISE

Take a moment to reflect deeply on the transformative influence of audacious goals. Recall a personal experience where setting lofty aspirations reshaped your understanding of success. Once you've identified this pivotal moment, take some time to meditate on it. Allow yourself to connect with the emotions and insights it evokes. Finally, when you feel ready, write down your reflections, capturing the essence of how this experience redefined your perception of success.

MY TRANSFORMATIONAL MOMENT

Reflecting on audacious goals, I recall a pivotal moment when I aimed for admission to a highly competitive post-graduate program. Though daunting at first, I recognized that pursuing this ambition redefined my understanding of success and uncovered my potential.

REFLECTION PROMPT

How can setting goals beyond conventional expectations lead to a more fulfilling and purpose-driven life?

INVENTIVE MINDSET ACTIVITY

If your audacious goals were a beacon, what extraordinary paths would they illuminate for your journey?

ELEVATED CONSCIOUSNESS ACTIVITY

Affirm your commitment to pursuing audacious goals. Reflect, write and speak an affirmation reinforcing your belief in your ability to reach extraordinary heights.

CINEMATIC INSPIRATION

"The Pursuit of Happyness" (2023) - Director: Terrell Lamont.

DESCRIPTION

In this compelling documentary, filmmaker Terrell Lamont explores the enduring impact of "The Pursuit of Happyness." Through interviews, behind-the-scenes footage, and personal stories, it highlights how the film's themes of hope and resilience resonate with audiences worldwide. The narrative features individuals who, like Chris Gardner, face significant challenges yet bravely pursue their dreams. Lamont's film not only celebrates the cultural significance of the original but also serves as an inspiring testament to the human spirit's capacity to overcome obstacles in the relentless quest for happiness.

How did the characters' experiences or choices resonate with your life journey, and what insights can you draw from your actions or dilemmas to enhance your personal growth?

In what ways did the themes or messages of the movie challenge your perspectives, beliefs, or assumptions about yourself and the world around you, and how can you integrate these reflections into your daily life to foster positive change?

LETTER TO MY AUTHENTIC SELF:
A CELEBRATION OF UNIQUENESS AND ASPIRATION

Craft a heartfelt letter to your most authentic self—the purest reflection of who you truly are and the person you strive to be. Pour out your thoughts, dreams, and aspirations, celebrating your uniqueness and embracing the journey toward your fullest potential.

Dear Authentic Self,

QUOTE FOR THE WEEK

"In the depth of darkness, focus on the glimmering light within;
it is during our darkest moments that our inner strength shines the brightest."
— Aristotle

SCRIPTURE FOR THE WEEK

"The Lord is near to the brokenhearted and saves the crushed in spirit."
Psalm 34:18 (NIV)

WEEK TWENTY NINE

Embracing Transformation: Navigating the Winds of Change

POWER STEPS THIS WEEK

Reflect on a recent change or transformation in your life. What positive outcomes emerged from this experience? Write down three specific ways this change has contributed to your personal growth and well-being.

Identify one actionable step you can take today to embrace further transformation in your life. This could be trying something new, setting a small goal, or adopting a positive mindset. Write down your plan and commit to taking that step.

TRANSCENDENCE WRITING EXERCISE

Explore the theme of resilience. Write about a dark moment when you discovered an inner light guiding you through adversity.

MY TRANSFORMATIONAL MOMENT

Amid personal loss, I received counseling and support for workplace trauma, allowing myself grace and a safe space to begin the healing process. This experience revealed my resilience and deepened my understanding of the interconnectedness of compassion and healing.

REFLECTION PROMPT

How can focusing on the light within during dark moments empower you to navigate challenges with grace and strength?

INVENTIVE MINDSET ACTIVITY

If your inner strength were a beacon, what challenges would it illuminate a path through today?

ELEVATED CONSCIOUSNESS ACTIVITY

Affirm your inner strength during difficult times by repeating a mantra that reinforces your ability to find light in darkness.

CINEMATIC INSPIRATION
"La La Land" (2016) - Directed by Damien Chazelle

DESCRIPTION
"La La Land" is a musical romantic drama that explores transformation and the inevitability of change. It follows aspiring actress Mia and jazz musician Sebastian as they chase their dreams in Los Angeles. Through vibrant musical numbers and poignant storytelling, the film celebrates the highs and lows of pursuing one's passions, emphasizing themes of ambition, love, and the journey of navigating life's changes.

How did the characters' experiences or choices resonate with your life journey, and what insights can you draw from your actions or dilemmas to enhance your personal growth?

\
\
\
\
\

In what ways did the themes or messages of the movie challenge your perspectives, beliefs, or assumptions about yourself and the world around you, and how can you integrate these reflections into your daily life to foster positive change?

LETTER TO MY AUTHENTIC SELF:
A CELEBRATION OF UNIQUENESS AND ASPIRATION

Craft a heartfelt letter to your most authentic self—the purest reflection of who you truly are and the person you strive to be. Pour out your thoughts, dreams, and aspirations, celebrating your uniqueness and embracing the journey toward your fullest potential.

Dear Authentic Self,

QUOTE FOR THE WEEK

"Venture into the unexplored, for it is in forging new paths that we discover the true essence of our journey."
— Ralph Waldo Emerson

SCRIPTURE FOR THE WEEK

"Your word is a lamp for my feet, a light on my path."
Psalm 119:105 (NIV)

WEEK THIRTY

Exploring the Uncharted: Discovering Essence in New Paths

POWER STEPS THIS WEEK

Identify an area of your life where you can venture into the unknown.

Take the first step towards exploring this uncharted territory.

TRANSCENDENCE WRITING EXERCISE

Reflect on the theme of exploration. Write about a time when stepping into the unknown led to personal growth and discovery.

MY TRANSFORMATIONAL MOMENT

A pivotal moment in my career arose from financial challenges that forced me to face uncertainty. Embracing this uncharted territory unlocked my hidden potential and creativity. By aligning my core values with my vision, I set clear goals to turn obstacles into opportunities for growth.

REFLECTION PROMPT

How can venturing beyond familiar paths lead to a more fulfilling and purpose-driven life?

INVENTIVE MINDSET ACTIVITY

If your life were a map, where would you mark the unexplored territories waiting to be discovered?

ELEVATED CONSCIOUSNESS ACTIVITY

Affirm your courage to tread new paths. Create and meditate on an affirming thought that reinforces your willingness to embrace the unexplored.

CINEMATIC INSPIRATION
"Inception" (2010) - Directed by Christopher Nolan

DESCRIPTION
"Inception" directed by Christopher Nolan, explores the complex relationship between dreams and reality through Dom Cobb and his team navigating layered dreamscapes. The film challenges perceptions and prompts reflection on existence, showcasing its transformative nature through stunning visuals and innovative storytelling.

How did the characters' experiences or choices resonate with your life journey, and what insights can you draw from your actions or dilemmas to enhance your personal growth?

In what ways did the themes or messages of the movie challenge your perspectives, beliefs, or assumptions about yourself and the world around you, and how can you integrate these reflections into your daily life to foster positive change?

LETTER TO MY AUTHENTIC SELF: A CELEBRATION OF UNIQUENESS AND ASPIRATION

Craft a heartfelt letter to your most authentic self—the purest reflection of who you truly are and the person you strive to be. Pour out your thoughts, dreams, and aspirations, celebrating your uniqueness and embracing the journey toward your fullest potential.

Dear Authentic Self,

QUOTE FOR THE WEEK

"Imagination is more important than knowledge. For knowledge is limited, whereas imagination embraces the entire world, stimulating progress, giving birth to evolution."
— Albert Einstein

SCRIPTURE FOR THE WEEK

"But it is the spirit in a person, the breath of the Almighty, that gives them understanding."
Job 32:8 (NIV)

WEEK THIRTY ONE

Unleashing Imagination: A Journey Beyond Boundaries

POWER STEPS THIS WEEK

Reflect on how imagination and divine insight shape your journey. Write about a dream that pushes your boundaries and how it could transform your future.

Identify three intentions to help you realize this dream. Focus on specific actions or mindset shifts that align with your vision and inner guidance.

TRANSCENDENCE WRITING EXERCISE

Explore a moment when your imagination led you to a breakthrough. Write about the experience, detailing the feelings and insights that emerged from this moment of creativity.

MY TRANSFORMATIONAL MOMENT

After a personal setback, I created this guided journal to channel my thoughts. Enrolling in workshops and classes rekindled my passion for learning, enhancing my writing and self-reflection while fostering personal growth.

REFLECTION PROMPT

Consider how your understanding of imagination has evolved throughout this journal. What new perspectives have you gained about its role in your personal and spiritual growth?

INVENTIVE MINDSET ACTIVITY

Engage in a creative brainstorming session. Set a timer for 10 minutes and write down as many ideas as possible related to your dreams. Don't censor yourself - let your imagination flow freely.

ELEVATED CONSCIOUSNESS ACTIVITY

Take a nature walk, allowing your mind to wander. As you walk, observe your surroundings and let your thoughts drift towards your dreams and aspirations. Take notes on any insights that arise during this time.

CINEMATIC INSPIRATION
"Field of Dreams" (1989) Directed by Phil Alden Robinson.

DESCRIPTION
Ray Kinsella, an Iowa farmer, builds a baseball field in his cornfield after hearing a mysterious voice. Despite skepticism, he follows his vision, leading to magical encounters and a deeper understanding of dreams and relationships. The film showcases the power of belief and the importance of pursuing one's vision against the odds.

How did the characters' experiences or choices resonate with your life journey, and what insights can you draw from your actions or dilemmas to enhance your personal growth?

In what ways did the themes or messages of the movie challenge your perspectives, beliefs, or assumptions about yourself and the world around you, and how can you integrate these reflections into your daily life to foster positive change?

LETTER TO MY AUTHENTIC SELF:
A CELEBRATION OF UNIQUENESS AND ASPIRATION

Craft a heartfelt letter to your most authentic self—the purest reflection of who you truly are and the person you strive to be. Pour out your thoughts, dreams, and aspirations, celebrating your uniqueness and embracing the journey toward your fullest potential.

Dear Authentic Self,

Guided Meditation

EMBRACING IMAGINATION

Find a quiet space to sit comfortably. Close your eyes and take a few deep breaths. Visualize a vibrant scene that represents your imagination. Allow yourself to explore this space, noticing the details and feelings it evokes. Spend 5-10 minutes immersing yourself in this imaginative world, letting it inspire your thoughts and aspirations.

CLOSING AFFIRMATION

"I unleash my imagination to explore limitless possibilities, embracing the journey beyond boundaries."

CLOSING THOUGHTS

As you conclude this 31-week journey, take a moment to reflect on the growth and transformation you've experienced. Embrace the power of your imagination as a vital tool for shaping your future. Remember, the journey continues beyond these pages, and your potential is limitless.

About the Author

SUDECIA BROWN an inspiring educator, minister, speaker, and author, has dedicated over two decades to uplifting others through her unwavering commitment to education and faith. Hailing from Boston, she seamlessly intertwines her passion for teaching with her deep-rooted dedication to personal growth and spiritual empowerment. Sudecia holds advanced degrees in Organizational Management and Educational Administration and is a proud alumni of the Trimm Institute for Global Leadership which demonstrates her unwavering dedication to her mission.

As a versatile educator, Sudecia has served in numerous roles, including Teacher, Inclusion Specialist/Operational Leader, Mentor, and Communication Strategist. Her leadership extends beyond the classroom. She founded the Brilliance Book Club, a global ministry uniting women across the United States, Bahamas and Africa, demonstrating her ability to connect and inspire across continents. She offers spiritual guidance through this platform, fosters meaningful discussions, and supports those in need.

Sudecia's book, Radiant Reflections: A 31-Week Journey to Illuminate Your Path of Growth and Transformation, is not just a guide but a personal testament to her resilience. It was born from a personal crisis, a journey she openly shares, making her book a powerful guide to self-discovery and transformation. Each day, readers are not just invited, they are encouraged to actively explore their inner strength and take deliberate steps toward a more inspired and intentional life.

Outside of her professional work, Sudecia finds solace and inspiration in nature, often taking long walks in her hometown of Boston. These moments of peace and clarity deeply influence her writing and reflections. She is passionate about connecting with her readers and warmly invites you to join her on this growth journey. Connect with Sudecia on social media or on LinkedIn to continue the conversation and explore more of her work.

www.ingramcontent.com/pod-product-compliance
Lightning Source LLC
Chambersburg PA
CBHW040237110526
44582CB00023B/222/J